*A*DVENT *and* *C*HRISTMAS *W*ISDOM
—— *from* ——
G. K. CHESTERTON

**Other titles in the
Advent and Christmas Wisdom series**

$\mathcal{A}$DVENT and $\mathcal{C}$HRISTMAS $\mathcal{W}$ISDOM
——— *from* ———
G. K. CHESTERTON

Daily Scripture and Prayers Together
With G. K. Chesterton's Own Words

The Center for the Study
of C. S. Lewis and Friends

Compilation, Prayers, and Actions by
Thom Satterlee and Robert Moore-Jumonville

Liguori
LIGUORI, MISSOURI

Imprimi Potest:
Thomas D. Picton, C.Ss.R.
Provincial, Denver Province
The Redemptorists

Published by Liguori Publications
Liguori, Missouri
www.liguori.org

Compilation, Prayers, and Actions by Thom Satterlee and
Robert Moore-Jumonville

Library of Congress Cataloging-in-Publication Data

Chesterton, G. K. (Gilbert Keith), 1874-1936.
    Advent and Christmas wisdom from G. K. Chesterton : daily scripture and prayers together with G. K. Chesterton's own words / compiled by Thom Satterlee and Robert Moore-Jumonville. — 1st ed.
        p. cm.
pISBN: 978-0-7648-1628-4
eISBN: 978-0-7648-6030-0
    1. Advent—Prayers and devotions. 2. Christmas—Prayers and devotion. I. Satterlee, Thom. II. Moore-Jumonville, Robert. III. Title.
    BV40.C46 2007
    242'.33—dc22

                                                                2007016843

Liguori Publications, a nonprofit corporation, is an apostolate of the Redemptorists. To learn more about the Redemptorists, visit Redemptorists.com.

Printed in the United States of America
17 16 15 14 13 / 7 6 5 4 3

$\mathcal{C}$ontents

Introduction

IF GILBERT KEITH CHESTERTON came striding across the
threshold of your fire-crackling Christmas party, you would most
likely gape in wonder, then laugh, listen, and come to love him.
He might remind you of Father Christmas grinning from ear to
ear, except for the cigar clenched in his mouth.

At a towering six-foot-four and weighing three hundred
pounds, Chesterton was energetic and alluring, a daunting giant,
whom strangers soon realized possessed the heart of an elf. He
played Christmas games with children, requesting colored tinsel
to paste on his own cutout cardboard figures. His contagious
laughter invited others to join him in his wit and repartee, his
childlike innocence, and love of life. In him was a humor akin
to humility: a humor that delighted in life but refused to take
the enigma of being human too seriously, a joyous humor with a
sane estimate of itself and others, a holy humor that lived lightly
because it trusted God for maintaining the universe.

Born in London in1874, and dying there in 1936, Chesterton
seemed a comic figure to some, but his towering intellect matched
his physical height. This was a man who could write a longhand
essay while simultaneously dictating another to his secretary.
Having studied art at the Slade School in London, Chesterton
humbly claimed his main craft as journalism. But in addition
to writing a weekly article for his entire adult life, Chesterton
authored more than a hundred books and contributed essays to

many more. Furthermore, he wrote capably and Christianly on almost every conceivable topic in almost every imaginable genre: literary criticism, poetry, novel, short story, biography, theology, apologetics, mystery—and the list goes on. Rather than journalist, he could be better dubbed a Christian cultural critic in the English "man of letters" tradition.

Chesterton delights many of his readers as a gracious person who fights for Christian truth, but never arrogantly, rather as a genius with an open mind, as a grateful person with deep devotion to God and commitment to stand alongside the common citizen. Perhaps you will come to find, as others before you, that Gilbert Keith Chesterton has walked into your life to make you laugh and think, to serve as your friend and mentor.

ROBERT MOORE-JUMONVILLE
SPRING ARBOR UNIVERSITY
2007

How to Use This Book

ADVENT—that period of great anticipatory joy—is a time of preparation for the celebration of Jesus' arrival in Bethlehem as a helpless infant. In the Western liturgy, Advent begins four Sundays prior to December 25—the Sunday closest to November 30, which is the feast of Saint Andrew, Jesus' first disciple.

The annual commemoration of Jesus' birth begins the Christmas cycle of the liturgical year—a cycle that runs from Christmas Eve to the Sunday after the feast of the Epiphany. In keeping with the unfolding of the message of the liturgical year, this book is designed to be used during the entire period from the First Sunday of Advent to the end of the Christmas cycle.

The four weeks of Advent are often thought of as symbolizing the four different ways that Jesus comes into the world: (1) at his birth as a helpless infant at Bethlehem, (2) at his arrival in the hearts of believers, (3) at his death, and (4) at his arrival on Judgment Day.

Because Christmas falls on a different day of the week each year, the fourth week of Advent is never really finished; it is abruptly, joyously, and solemnly abrogated by the annual coming again of Jesus at Christmas. Christ's Second Coming will also one day abruptly interrupt our sojourn here on earth.

Since the calendar dictates the number of days in Advent, this book includes Scripture and meditation readings for a full twenty-eight days. These twenty-eight daily readings make up

Part I of this book. It is suggested that the reader begin at the beginning and, on Christmas, switch to Part II, which contains materials for the twelve days of Christmas. If there are any "extra" entries from Part I, these may be read by doubling up days, if so desired, or by reading two entries on weekends. Alternately, one may just skip these entries that do not fit within the Advent time frame for that particular year.

Each "day" in this book begins with the words of G. K. Chesterton taken from various sources as acknowledged on pages 113 and 114. Following that quotation is an excerpt from Scripture, which is related in some way to the beginning quote. Next is provided a small prayer, also built on the ideas from the two preceding passages. Finally, an Advent or Christmas activity is suggested as a way to apply the messages to one's daily life.

Part III of this book proposes two optional formats for using each day as part of a longer liturgical observance similar to Night Prayer combined with a version of the Office of Readings. These options are for those who may wish to use this book as part of a more-developed individual or group observance. The purpose of these readings is to enrich the Advent/Christmas/Epiphany season of the liturgical year and set up a means by which individuals, families, or groups may observe the true meaning of the season.

PART I

~~~~~~~~

READINGS *for* ADVENT

DAY 1

The Gift of Hope

*I*t is currently said that hope goes with youth, and lends to youth its wings of a butterfly; but I fancy that hope is the last gift given to man, and the only gift not given to youth. Youth is pre-eminently the period in which a man can be lyric, fanatical, poetic; but youth is the period in which a man can be hopeless. The end of every episode is the end of the world. But the power of hoping through everything, the knowledge that the soul survives its adventures, that great inspiration comes to the middle-aged; God has kept that good wine until now. It is from the backs of the elderly gentlemen that the wings of the butterfly should burst.

CHARLES DICKENS: LAST OF THE GREAT MEN

HOPE IN THE GOSPEL

In our prayers for you we always thank God, the Father of our Lord Jesus Christ, for we have heard of your faith in Christ Jesus and of the love that you have for all the saints, because of the hope laid up for you in heaven. You have heard of this hope before in the word of the truth, the gospel that has come to you. Just as it is bearing fruit and growing in the whole world, so it has been bearing fruit among yourselves from the day you heard it and truly comprehended the grace of God.

COLOSSIANS 1:3–6

PRAYER

God of hope, Giver of hope, help us in our hopeless moments. Turn our hearts and minds to the promise of the gospel, to your dear Son, Jesus Christ. Strengthen our faith in what we have heard. Especially in our troubles, remind us of our true home with you in heaven. Help us to hope for eternal life with you.

ADVENT ACTION

Make a list of the things you are currently hoping for. This may include advancement in your career, the success of an important relationship, the completion of a project, or any number of things. When you have finished the list, look over it. Circle one item and say a brief prayer for God's help in bringing this about. If praying feels uncomfortable, consider whether the item you have chosen is something you should hope for. Ask God for clarity. Resolve to hope for those things that bring you closest to God.

Delightful Bulbous Heads

*T*he fascination of children lies in this: that with each of them all things are remade, and the universe is put again upon its trial. As we walk the streets and see below us those delightful bulbous heads, three times too big for the body...we ought always primarily to remember that within every one of these heads there is a new universe, as new as it was on the seventh day of creation. In each of those orbs there is a new system of stars, new grass, new cities, a new sea.

THE DEFENDANT

LITTLE CHILDREN

Jesus said, "Let the little children come to me, and do not stop them; for it is to such as these that the kingdom of heaven belongs." And he laid his hands on them and went on his way.

MATTHEW 19:14–15

PRAYER

Jesus, you loved children and welcomed them to you. Help us to find their qualities in ourselves—the wonder, the openness, the delight in living—and we will offer you thanks for the love you fill us with. May we, too, walk in the kingdom of heaven.

ADVENT ACTION

If you are around children today, observe their behavior. Consider why Christ said that the kingdom of heaven belongs to them. As Christ laid his hands on the children, look for a way that you can show gentleness to a child. What word of encouragement might you speak? What obligation can you give up to spend time with a child?

DAY 3

Soaking in Solitude

I can recall in my childhood the continuous excitement of long days in which nothing happened; and an indescribable sense of fullness in large and empty rooms. And with whatever I retain of childishness (and whether it be a weakness or otherwise, I think I retain more than most) I still feel a very strong and positive pleasure in being stranded in queer and quiet places in neglected corners where nothing happens and anything may happen; in unfashionable hotels, in empty waiting-rooms, or in watering-places out of the season. It seems as if we needed such places, and sufficient solitude in them, to let certain nameless suggestions soak into us and make a richer soil for the subconsciousness.

ON "THE THRILLS OF BOREDOM," *ALL IS GRIST*

QUIET MY SOUL

O LORD, my heart is not lifted up,
my eyes are not raised too high;
I do not occupy myself with things
too great and too marvelous for me.
But I have calmed and quieted my soul,
like a weaned child with its mother;
my soul is like the weaned child that is with me.

O Israel, hope in the LORD
from this time on and forevermore.

PSALM 131

PRAYER

Lord, I am weak. I am distracted. I am restless. Unless you intervene, Lord, I shall always be this way. Give me, Lord, greater thirst for you—that I might love you in all things and above all things; that I might still my soul in your presence; that I might stay quiet long enough for you to whisper to me. Give me your peace, Lord, your peace that the world cannot comprehend.

ADVENT ACTION

Try some form of contemplative prayer this week. One way is to choose a word that reflects what you feel you need from God right now (one syllable is best): *peace, love, strength.* Get comfortable in a quiet place where you will not be disturbed. When thoughts come crashing in, repeat the word silently to yourself as a symbol of your intention to sit adoringly in God's presence. The point is not to "get" something out of this time of silence, though you may find yourself more relaxed afterward. One of the main functions of contemplative prayer is spiritual detoxification: letting go of the junk that clogs our souls. Try the one word (centering prayer) method for a few days. Another option is to focus on a mental image (or icon). A third option is to repeat slowly and lovingly the Jesus Prayer (either silently or aloud): "Lord Jesus Christ, have mercy on me."

DAY 4

Fundamental Fact of Being

There is at the back of all our lives an abyss of light, more blinding and unfathomable than any abyss of darkness; and it is the abyss of actuality, of existence, of the fact that things truly are, and that we ourselves are incredibly and sometimes almost incredulously real. It is the fundamental fact of being, as against not being; it is unthinkable, yet we cannot unthink it, though we may sometimes be unthinking about it; unthinking and especially unthanking. For he who has realized this reality knows that it does outweigh, literally to infinity, all lesser regrets or arguments for negation, and that under all our grumblings there is a subconscious substance of gratitude.

CHAUCER

In the Beginning

In the beginning was the Word, and the Word was with God, and the Word was God. He was in the beginning with God. All things came into being through him, and without him not one thing came into being. What has come into being in him was life, and the life was the light of all people. The light shines in the darkness, and the darkness did not overcome it.

JOHN 1:1–5

Prayer

Lord Jesus, you are the light that shines in the darkness. Remind us to turn to you, to call out to you, when we feel we're being swallowed by darkness, by doubts, by troubles and frustrations. Thank you for the very fact of our being.

Advent Action

Chesterton tells us that "under all our grumblings there is a subconscious substance of gratitude." Pay attention to the remarks you make to family, friends, and coworkers today. Try to turn one would-be grumble into an occasion for thanks.

Appreciation

The aim of life is appreciation; there is no sense in not appreciating things; and there is no sense in having more of them if you have less appreciation of them.

AUTOBIOGRAPHY

LEARNING CONTENTMENT

I have learned to be content with whatever I have. I know what it is to have little, and I know what it is to have plenty. In any and all circumstances I have learned the secret of being well-fed and of going hungry, of having plenty and of being in need. I can do all things through him who strengthens me.

PHILIPPIANS 4:11b–13

PRAYER

Lord, may we learn what it means to appreciate what we do have instead of constantly stewing over what we do not have. Teach us this secret of contentment that Chesterton and the Apostle Paul knew so well.

ADVENT ACTION

Find an ordinary object that you already own and truly value. The object may be as commonplace as a handbag or pair of boots, as homey as a basket or bowl, as symbolic as a book or soccer ball. Place this object as the centerpiece on your table or in a prominent place where you will notice it frequently. Each time it comes to your attention, consider a new way of appreciating it, thanking God for its qualities and the joy it brings you.

DAY 6

Illumination of Our Souls

*A*ll ceremony depends on symbol; and all symbols have been vulgarized and made stale by the commercial conditions of our time....Of all these faded and falsified symbols, the most melancholy example is the ancient symbol of the flame. In every civilized age and country, it has been a natural thing to talk of some great festival on which "the town was illuminated." There is no meaning nowadays in saying the town was illuminated.... The whole town is illuminated already, but not for noble things. It is illuminated solely to insist on the immense importance of trivial and material things, blazoned from motives entirely mercenary....It has not destroyed the difference between light and darkness, but it has allowed the lesser light to put out the greater....Our streets are in a permanent dazzle, and our minds in a permanent darkness.

"THE RITUALS OF CHRISTMAS,"
THE ILLUSTRATED LONDON NEWS, DECEMBER 24, 1927

Sitting in Spiritual Shadows

"The people who sat in darkness have seen a great light, and for those who sat in the region and shadow of death light has dawned."

Matthew 4:16

Prayer

O God, who declared "Let light shine out of darkness" (2 Corinthians 4:6), let your light burn bright in our hearts and homes this Advent. Attract us to the true light of Christ and give us aversion to the impostors. Help us see past the season's tinsel. Above all, let us not be afraid when your light shines in the dark corners of our souls, exposing what is broken and ailing. May your light bring healing and wholeness.

Advent Action

Begin a tradition this year with a candle. Each day this week, allow your house first to become dark. Then light a single candle and read the verse from Matthew above. Remain attentively silent for one or two minutes. Close by thanking God for the light of Christ. The whole ritual need take no longer than five minutes; the daily repetition is what will add meaning to this exercise.

DAY 7

Praise

*M*an is more himself, man is more manlike, when joy is the fundamental thing in him, and grief the superficial. Melancholy should be an innocent interlude, a tender and fugitive frame of mind; praise should be the permanent pulsation of the soul.

ORTHODOXY

DOXOLOGY

> *Praise the LORD!*
> *Praise God in his sanctuary;*
> *   praise him in his mighty firmament!*
> *Praise him for his mighty deeds;*
> *   praise him according to his surpassing greatness!*

Praise him with trumpet sound;
   praise him with lute and harp!
Praise him with tambourine and dance;
   praise him with strings and pipe!
Praise him with clanging cymbals;
   praise him with loud clashing cymbals!
Let everything that breathes praise the LORD!
Praise the LORD!

PSALM 150

PRAYER

Lord of All Breathing Things, may we join in the chorus of praise, knowing that joy is our most natural state and that you are The One Most Worthy to Be Praised.

ADVENT ACTION

Where do you praise God? For what reasons do you praise God? Make a list of the places and reasons for your praise and add one or two new ones that would increase your overall praise of him.

DAY 8

Too Busy to Wake Up

*J*don't drink or smoke, you know," he said irrelevantly, "because I think they're drugs. And yet I fancy all hobbies, like my camera and bicycle, are drugs too....Drugging myself with speed, and sunshine, and fatigue, and fresh air. Pedalling [sic] the machine so fast that I turn into a machine myself. That's the matter with all of us. We're too busy to wake up."

INGLEWOOD, IN *MANALIVE*

WHAT TIME IS IT?

Besides this, you know what time it is, how it is now the moment for you to wake from sleep. For salvation is nearer to us now than when we became believers; the night is far gone, the day is near. Let us then lay aside the works of darkness and put on the armor of light.

ROMANS 13:11–12

PRAYER

Too easily, Lord of Light, we curry the convenient slumber of consumerism. We rush headlong in a hurry to entertain ourselves asleep so we feel unconstrained to love. Wake us gently, gracious God, a little more each day, that with all your saints we might live our lives spiritually alert, more fully aware of your sustaining and guiding presence.

ADVENT ACTION

Wear your watch or your favorite bracelet on your opposite hand today (or, if you are very brave, wear mismatching socks or something outrageously garish). The point, of course, is to awaken you spiritually, to remind you that every moment the eternal intersects the temporal. When you do notice your subtle (or outlandish) "act of devotion," recite this simple sentence prayer: "Lord, awaken me to your loving presence."

DAY 9

A Merry Christmas

*I*t is a mere fact of English history that the idea of a Merry Christmas was maintained much more faithfully by the ragged carol-singers than it was by the Merry Gentlemen to whom they sang their carols. The Merry Gentlemen were disposed to become decidedly Dismal Gentlemen in the Puritan terror of the seventeenth century. It was among the populace that Christmas was suppressed with difficulty; many of the political squires, and nearly all the merchant princes, lent their aid to suppress it. Christmas had only survived so late as that by the loyalty and tenacity of peasants and other poor men. And, if poor men could keep Christmas, surely we can keep Christmas as if we were poor men.

"ON THE CHRISTMAS TRADITIONS OF THE POOR,"
ILLUSTRATED LONDON NEWS, DECEMBER 29, 1917

OUR POOR FORTUNE

Then [Jesus] looked up at his disciples and said:
"Blessed are you who are poor,
for yours is the kingdom of God.
"Blessed are you who are hungry now,
for you will be filled.
"Blessed are you who weep now,
for you will laugh."

LUKE 6:20–21

PRAYER

Lord, our culture runs from poverty as if it were the plague. We try so hard to convince ourselves that we are safe and sheltered. Show us, Teacher, that we are only secure as long as our lives are grounded in you. Teach us to abide in you, to hold all our possessions loosely—as stewards who received a trust from you—to put all you have blessed us with back into your hands each morning. Free our hearts for generosity. Give us opportunity to serve the poor—especially by granting them respect, dignity, and love.

Advent Action

Once an acquaintance told me how when he was poor the main Christmas present his children would receive was a box of cereal. Each child could go to the store and pick their favorite brand. To this day, he declared, everyone in the family still received a box of cereal under the tree—as a reminder of when they were poor and as a reminder that God befriends the poor. Find some object that represents either a time in your life when you were poor or a place in your life where your "good fortune" is vulnerable today—a life insurance policy, a book from college days, an early wedding present, a picture of a loved one who has died. Place the article prominently in your home as an object for meditation and spiritual reflection.

A Freer Sky

How much larger your life would be if your self could become smaller in it; if you could really look at other men with common curiosity and pleasure; if you could see them walking as they are in their sunny selfishness and their virile indifference! You would begin to be interested in them, because they were not interested in you. You would break out of this tiny and tawdry theatre in which your own little plot is always played, and you would find yourself under a freer sky, in a street full of splendid strangers.

ORTHODOXY

THE INTERESTS OF OTHERS

Do nothing from selfish ambition or conceit, but in humility regard others as better than yourselves. Let each of you look not to your own interests, but to the interests of others. Let the same mind be in you that was in Christ Jesus,
who, though he was in the form of God,
did not regard equality with God
as something to be exploited,
but emptied himself,
taking the form of a slave,
being born in human likeness.

PHILIPPIANS 2:3–7

PRAYER

Most humble Lord Jesus, you taught us through your incarnation the meaning of caring for others. There is in you no conceit or ambition; in you there is only love for others and a desire to serve. We passionately desire to follow your example. Help us, we pray, to care for others as you cared for us. Just as you took on our human form to serve us, may we take on the concerns of others and, like you, gladly become slaves to their needs.

ADVENT ACTION

Find a public place where you can sit alone for about fifteen minutes. While sitting there, look around at the others and imagine their lives, their cares, their dreams. Through your imagination, try to draw closer to these strangers and further away from yourself. Before you leave, reread the wonderful passage from Chesterton on page 22.

DAY 11

Homeless in Our Homes

The Christmas season is domestic; and for that reason most people now prepare for it by struggling in tramcars, standing in queues, rushing away in trains, crowding despairingly into teashops, and wondering when or whether they will ever get home. I do not know whether some of them disappear for ever in the toy department or simply lie down and die in the tea-rooms; but by the look of them, it is quite likely. Just before the great festival of the home the whole population seems to have become homeless.

THE THING: WHY I AM A CATHOLIC

RETURNING AND REST

For thus said the Lord GOD, the Holy One of Israel:
In returning and rest you shall be saved;
    in quietness and in trust shall be your strength.
But you refused and said,
"No! We will flee upon horses"—
    therefore you shall flee!
and, "We will ride upon swift steeds"—
    therefore your pursuers shall be swift!
A thousand shall flee at the threat of one,
    at the threat of five you shall flee,
until you are left
    like a flagstaff on the top of a mountain,
    like a signal on a hill.

Therefore the LORD waits to be gracious to you;
    therefore he will rise up to show mercy to you.
For the LORD is a God of justice;
    blessed are all those who wait for him.

ISAIAH 30:15–18

PRAYER

Lord, rescue us from getting sucked into the cyclone of a commercialized Christmas this year. Help! Save us! Help us commit more earnestly to times of prayer, worship, silence, and reflection. Convince us to trade commotion for community and frenzy for friends. Show us what it takes to become more genuinely human that we might recognize You within us and your face in the face of others.

Be radical: stay home this year. Look at your calendar early and block out segments of sanity. When someone asks or makes demands on your time, simply reply, "I'm sorry, but we/I have something already scheduled." Just say no. Remember, if this holy season turns out as crazy as previous years, it was at least partly your choice. Determine, instead, to be copartners with God in writing your own future. If you want to be even more radical, unplug. Block out days, or parts of days, where you fast from electronics: no television or DVDs; no music or radio; no computer. Instead, talk, play games, cook, do crafts, exercise, read, pray.

DAY 12

Levity and Levitation

*A*ngels can fly because they can take themselves lightly. This has always been the instinct of Christendom, and especially the instinct of Christian art. Remember how Fra Angelico represented all his angels, not only as birds, but almost as butterflies. Remember how the most earnest medieval art was full of light and fluttering draperies, of quick and capering feet....In the old Christian pictures the sky over every figure is like a blue or gold parachute. Every figure seems ready to fly up and float about in the heavens. The tattered cloak of the beggar will bear him up like the rayed plumes of the angels. But the kings in their heavy gold and the proud in their robes of purple will all of their nature sink downwards, for pride cannot rise to levity or levitation. Pride is the downward drag of all things into an easy solemnity. One "settles down" into a sort of selfish seriousness; but one has to rise to a gay self-forgetfulness. A man "falls" into a brown study; he reaches up at a blue sky.

ORTHODOXY

REVIVE THE SPIRIT

For thus says the high and lofty one
   who inhabits eternity, whose name is Holy:
I dwell in the high and holy place,
   and also with those who are contrite and humble in spirit,
to revive the spirit of the humble,
   and to revive the heart of the contrite.

ISAIAH 57:15

PRAYER

Holy God, bear us upward toward you. Make our spirits lighter, more joyful. Teach us how to live without fretting, without the anxieties that so often obscure our view of you in your high and holy place, that heaven which is our true home.

ADVENT ACTION

If you live near an art museum, plan a day trip there and spend an hour or more in the Medieval section. If not, find art books at a local library or search the Internet for images of great art. As you look at the paintings, consider what Chesterton says about the lightness, the "gay self-forgetfulness" of some of the figures. Try to appreciate the art while also opening yourself to it as a mode for devotion.

DAY 13

Trading Mirth for Madness

*Y*ou cannot be too solemn about golf to be a good golfer; you can be a great deal too solemn about Christianity to be a good Christian. You may put into your neckties solemnity, and nothing but solemnity, because neckties are not the whole of your life—at least, I hope not. But in anything that does cover the whole of your life—in your philosophy and your religion—you must have mirth. If you do not have mirth you will certainly have madness.

LUNACY AND LETTERS

HUMILITY

For by the grace given to me I say to everyone among you not to think of yourself more highly than you ought to think, but to think with sober judgment, each according to the measure of faith that God has assigned.

ROMANS 12:3

PRAYER

Grant us, O God who hung the stars, a holy sense of humor akin to humility; that having a sane estimate of who we are in Christ and who Christ is as your Son, we might allow ourselves and others to try and to fail. Let us walk humbly today. And let humility grow in us habits of patience, kindness, and love—love that is not irritable, or arrogant, or resentful, or rude.

ADVENT ACTION

Bless someone this week for the love of Christ through an act of service done in kindness and humility. Take out the trash every night; fix something for someone; rake leaves or shovel snow for a neighbor; offer to baby-sit for a friend. Smile while you work—especially at yourself. While you are "doing your good deed," repeat a Christmas verse or a line from a carol as a prayer.

DAY 14

The Camel and the Needle

I know that the most modern manufacture has been really occupied in trying to produce an abnormally large needle. I know that the most recent biologists have been chiefly anxious to discover a very small camel. But if we diminish the camel to his smallest, or open the eye of the needle to its largest—if, in short, we assume the words of Christ to have meant the very least that they could mean, His words must at the very least mean this—that rich men are not very likely to be morally trustworthy....There is one thing that Christ and all the Christian saints have said with a sort of savage monotony. They have said simply that to be rich is to be in peculiar danger of moral wreck.

ORTHODOXY

NOTHING IS IMPOSSIBLE WITH GOD

Then Jesus looked around and said to his disciples, "How hard it will be for those who have wealth to enter the kingdom of God!" And the disciples were perplexed at these words. But Jesus said to them again, "Children, how hard it is to enter the kingdom of God! It is easier for a camel to go through the eye of a needle than for someone who is rich to enter the kingdom of God." They were greatly astounded and said to one another, "Then who can be saved?" Jesus looked at them and said, "For mortals it is impossible, but not for God; for God all things are possible."

MARK 10:23–27

PRAYER

Jesus, you spoke hard words about the rich young ruler. We confess that we are too much like him; together we form a camel train trudging toward the tiniest needle, its speck of an eye. How can we hope to pass through into the kingdom of God? We rely on you, God of the Impossible, and not ourselves. Make us into what you would have us be.

ADVENT ACTION

Once when she was asked how much money a person should give away, Mother Teresa answered that we should give until it hurts—and then give some more. You can imagine what a camel would feel like trying to squeeze through the eye of the needle. Perhaps our giving should create commensurate pain. Take a moment and think about the charitable giving that you have done this year. What more can you give away, even after it hurts you?

DAY 15

Chrysanthemums or Billiards?

$\mathcal{C}$hrist commanded us to have love for all men, but even if we had equal love for all men, to speak of having the same love for all men is merely bewildering nonsense. If we love a man at all, the impression he produces on us must be vitally different to the impression produced by another man whom we love. To speak of having the same kind of regard for both is about as sensible as asking a man whether he prefers chrysanthemums or billiards. Christ did not love humanity; He never said He loved humanity; He loved men. Neither He nor anyone else can love humanity; it is like loving a gigantic centipede.

VARIED TYPES

LOVE ONE ANOTHER

"I give you a new commandment, that you love one another. Just as I have loved you, you also should love one another. By this everyone will know that you are my disciples, if you have love for one another."

JOHN 13:34–35

PRAYER

Lord Jesus, Great Role Model of Love, help us to love as you did, sacrificially and personally. Show us those individuals whom you would have us love, today, right now. Shake us from our routine selfishness and give us the desire to help others. May we follow your new commandment to love one another. Let us be your true disciples, we pray.

ADVENT ACTION

When you prayed the prayer above, did a certain name enter your mind? Have you thought of an individual who would benefit from your love today? If so, spend a few moments thinking of a specific act you can do for that person. It may be as simple as doing the dishes, writing a card, or taking time to meet with the person and playing the role of listener or giver.

DAY 16

Big Bad Shops

$\mathcal{J}$ think the big shop is a bad shop. I think it bad not only in a moral but a mercantile sense; that is, I think shopping there is not only a bad action but a bad bargain. I think the monster emporium is not only vulgar and insolent, but incompetent and uncomfortable; and I deny that its large organization is efficient. Large organization is loose organization. Nay, it would be almost as true to say that organization is always disorganization....I need not dwell on the other and still more entertaining claims made for the colossal combination of departments. One of the funniest is the statement that it is convenient to get everything in the shop. That is to say, it is convenient to walk the length of the street, so long as you walk indoors, or more frequently underground, instead of walking the same distance in the open air from one little shop to another. The truth is that the monopolist's shops are really convenient—to the monopolist. They have all the advantage of concentrating business as they concentrate wealth, in fewer and fewer of the citizens....My general thesis [is] that small properties should be revived.

"THE BLUFF OF THE BIG SHOPS," OUTLINE OF SANITY

TREASURE FOR THE FUTURE

As for those who in the present age are rich, command them not to be haughty, or to set their hopes on the uncertainty of riches, but rather on God who richly provides us with everything for our enjoyment. They are to do good, to be rich in good works, generous, and ready to share, thus storing up for themselves the treasure of a good foundation for the future, so that they may take hold of the life that really is life.

1 TIMOTHY 6:17–19

PRAYER

Lord, help us resolve to avoid all the craziness of what someone dubbed "Hallowthankmas"—that long period of consumer frenzy that begins long before Halloween and ends after the New Year with an emptiness and exhaustion that depletes our souls. Show us where we can simplify our lives, creating more time to meditate, pray, and play. Grant us, wise Lord, the gift of sanity this Advent and Christmas.

ADVENT ACTION

Consider how you might be able to shop and buy locally this year. Perhaps you can even make some of your own gifts. Consider also ways you might use the assets God has given you to bless others; practice giving things away.

DAY 17

The Force of Gravity

*S*eriousness is not a virtue. It would be a heresy, but a much more sensible heresy, to say that seriousness is a vice. It is really a natural trend or lapse into taking one's self gravely, because it is the easiest thing to do. It is much easier to write a good *Times* leading article than a good joke in *Punch*. For solemnity flows out of men naturally; but laughter is a leap. It is easy to be heavy: hard to be light. Satan fell by the force of gravity.

ORTHODOXY

CHEER UP

> *Anxiety weighs down the human heart,*
> *but a good word cheers it up.*

PROVERBS 12:25

PRAYER

God of Good Sense, you tell us in your word that we should not be anxious. But we take ourselves too seriously; we wear ourselves down from fretting. True freedom comes in serving you, and with that freedom comes joy. Remind us to cheer up. And help us to spread joy to our neighbors.

ADVENT ACTION

Find some time to just relax today. Watch a comic movie, read the funny pages, take your pet on a walk, ride your bike in the park, or build a snowman. Whatever you choose to do, try to not think about your cares. If a care does come to mind, say a brief prayer asking Jesus to help you with his command not to fret about your life.

DAY 18

The Doctrine of Conditional Joy

*F*or the pleasure of pedantry I will call it the Doctrine of Conditional Joy....The note of the fairy utterance always is, "You may live in a palace of gold and sapphire, *if* you do not say the word 'cow'"; or "You may live happily with the King's daughter, *if* you do not show her an onion." The vision always hangs upon a veto. All the dizzy and colossal things conceded depend upon one small thing withheld. All the wild and whirling things that are let loose depend upon one thing that is forbidden.

ORTHODOXY

BLESSED RESTRAINT

> *Happy are those*
> > *who do not follow the advice of the wicked,*
> *or take the path that sinners tread,*
> > *or sit in the seat of scoffers;*

but their delight is in the law of the LORD,
*   and on his law they meditate day and night.*
They are like trees
*   planted by streams of water,*
which yield their fruit in its season,
*   and their leaves do not wither.*
In all that they do, they prosper.

PSALM 1:1–3

PRAYER

Lord, Giver of All Good Gifts, we confess that we are crammed full, spiritually stuffed and fat because we never say no. Our frenetic rush to force more fun into our lives leaves us only increasingly empty. Give us the gift this Advent of self-restraint that we might be freed from distractions, addictions, and undue attachments—freer to love you and neighbor.

ADVENT ACTION

Self-restraint presents potential for deep joy. Identify the one "luxury" in your life right now you depend on most for comfort (what is it you think most about?). For some of us it is coffee, chocolate, or alcohol. For others it may be more subtle (popularity) or more insidious (power). Whatever this is you are depending on, fast from it this week for at least two days, calling out to God to fill you with his Spirit of joy whenever you notice it missing.

DAY 19

Expect Nothing, Enjoy Everything

It is commonly in a somewhat cynical sense that men have said, "Blessed is he that expecteth nothing, for he shall not be disappointed." It was in a wholly happy and enthusiastic sense that Saint Francis said, "Blessed is he that expecteth nothing, for he shall enjoy everything." It was by this deliberate idea of starting from zero, from the dark nothingness of his own deserts, that he did come to enjoy them.

SAINT FRANCIS OF ASSISI

THE GIFT OF GOD

This is what I have seen to be good: it is fitting to eat and drink and find enjoyment in all the toil with which one toils under the sun the few days of the life God gives us; for this is our lot. Likewise all to whom God gives wealth and possessions and whom he enables to enjoy them, and to accept their lot and find enjoyment in their toil—this is the gift of God. For they will scarcely brood over the days of their lives, because God keeps them occupied with the joy of their hearts.

ECCLESIASTES 5:18–20

PRAYER

Lord, our days are short, but we have done nothing to deserve even the few years of life that you give us. Teach us to be grateful for small things—food and drink and work—by remembering your servant Saint Francis, who truly expected nothing and enjoyed everything he had.

ADVENT ACTION

Each time you sit down to eat today, pause a little longer than you normally do. Meditate on the words from Ecclesiastes, "it is fitting to eat and drink and find enjoyment." Allow yourself to fill with thanks, to be thank-full.

DAY 20

Grateful

*T*he test of all happiness is gratitude; and I felt grateful, though I hardly knew to whom.

Children are grateful when Santa Claus puts in their stockings gifts of toys or sweets. Could I not be grateful to Santa Claus when he put in my stockings the gift of two miraculous legs? We thank people for birthday presents of cigars and slippers.

Can I thank no one for the birthday present of birth?

ORTHODOXY

GRATITUDE FOR SHEER EXISTENCE

O LORD, how manifold are your works!
In wisdom you have made them all;
the earth is full of your creatures.

These all look to you
to give them their food in due season;
when you give to them, they gather it up;
when you open your hand, they are filled with good
things.
When you hide your face, they are dismayed;
when you take away their breath, they die
and return to their dust.
When you send forth your spirit, they are created;
and you renew the face of the ground.

PSALM 104:24, 27–30

PRAYER

Lord, perhaps we are not happier right now because we live life without gratitude. We fret frenetically about what we do not have, thus poisoning our appreciation for what we do have. If we were more attentive to the miracles of legs, hands, eyes, ears, and breath—more alert to our very life—perhaps then we could begin to fathom the gifts of sweets and slippers and give proper thanks. Thank you, God, for everything.

ADVENT ACTION

If you keep a journal, list the chief four or five things for which you are grateful today. Now imagine that this day were the only day you were granted to live: what would you most appreciate? Demonstrate your gratitude through some creative act offered to God. Sculpt, draw, or paint a picture; write a poem or story; dance or sing a song. As you allow this act of worship to flower, remember, it is not the quality of the finished product that counts, but your expression of love from a sincere heart. God receives our gifts as we would from our own wide-eyed children. If appropriate, display your finished work somewhere prominently in your home where you can reflect on it as a grateful offering to God.

DAY 21

Giving Thanks

The great saint may be said to mix all his thoughts with thanks. All goods look better when they look like gifts.

SAINT FRANCIS OF ASSISI

IN ALL CIRCUMSTANCES, GIVE THANKS

[G]ive thanks in all circumstances; for this is the will of God in Christ Jesus for you.

1 THESSALONIANS 5:18

PRAYER

Lord, it is not always easy for us to give you thanks. Teach us, we pray. Teach us to thank you when we would rather grumble. Teach us to see all that we have as gifts from you. Forgive our ungratefulness. May our first and last thoughts be thoughts mixed with thanks.

ADVENT ACTION

Pick a number between ten and twenty. As you go through your day, identify reasons to give thanks to God until you reach your number. If you reach your number early in the day, try for a larger number.

DAY 22

To Believe or Not to Believe

*T*he...legend about Santa Claus coming down the chimney and the child hanging up the stocking raises the whole question which moderns least understand. It is that which Matthew Arnold called by a rather clumsy German word for "extra-belief"—all that fringe of mere fancy that is attached to faith, and yet is detachable from it.

"THE NEW ATTACK ON CHRISTMAS,"
ILLUSTRATED LONDON NEWS, DECEMBER 27, 1919

Personally, of course, I believe in Santa Claus; but it is the season of forgiveness, and I will forgive others for not doing so.

"THE RED ANGEL," *TREMENDOUS TRIFLES* 106

KNOWING WHAT IS IN US

When he was in Jerusalem during the Passover festival, many believed in his name because they saw the signs that he was doing. But Jesus on his part would not entrust himself to them, because he knew all people and needed no one to testify about anyone; for he himself knew what was in everyone.

JOHN 2:23–25

PRAYER

Father, forgive our unbelief. Forgive us for so easily forgetting. We wake up, perhaps we pray in the morning; and then we go about our external lives as though the spiritual world did not exist. We do our business as usual, pursuing our goals without you. Forgive us, too, for our indifference; for those times we know you are prompting us by your Spirit to learn of you or to love our neighbor, but we turn away the eyes of our heart. Take away our icy winter spirit. Put a new and right soul within us. We believe, Lord, help our unbelief.

ADVENT ACTION

Arrange to meet with a trusted friend or family member this week, someone who both knows you and has your best interests in mind. Ask the person to reflect back to you the current quality of your faith. Have them answer for you some of the following questions. Do you rationalize, avoid spiritual growth, or tend to blame others? Are there habits of selfishness or sin that you need to relinquish? Are there steps toward spiritual growth or maturity that God is calling you to take? Confess to this person any lack of faith that surfaces and ask him or her to pray for your spiritual restoration and revitalization.

DAY 23

What It's All About

People are losing the power to enjoy Christmas through identifying it with enjoyment. When once they lose sight of the old suggestion that it is all about something, they naturally fall into blank pauses of wondering what it is all about. To be told to rejoice on Christmas Day is reasonable and intelligible, if you understand the name, or even look at the word. To be told to rejoice on the twenty-fifth of December is like being told to rejoice at quarter-past eleven on Thursday week. You cannot suddenly be frivolous unless you believe there is a serious reason for being frivolous.

"THE NEW WAR ON CHRISTMAS," *G. K.'S WEEKLY*,
DECEMBER 26, 1925, QUOTED IN *BRAVE NEW FAMILY*

THE FULLNESS OF GOD

He is the image of the invisible God, the firstborn of all creation; for in him all things in heaven and on earth were created, things visible and invisible, whether thrones or dominions or rulers or powers—all things have been created through him and for him. He himself is before all things, and in him all things hold together. He is the head of the body, the church; he is the beginning, the firstborn from the dead, so that he might come to have first place in everything. For in him all the fullness of God was pleased to dwell, and through him God was pleased to reconcile to himself all things, whether on earth or in heaven, by making peace through the blood of his cross.

COLOSSIANS 1:15–20

PRAYER

Lord, the Advent and Christmas stories are so deep, their symbols are so rich, and carry such potential for nourishing our faith. Prevent us from adulterating the message with so many cultural accumulations that we lose sight of the heart of Christmas as worship.

ADVENT ACTION

Chesterton insisted, "There is not anything that signifies nothing." Look through your home, noticing some of the main Christmas symbols (Advent calendar and wreath; tree and ornaments; colors of green and red; lights, candles, foods, and traditions). If you have access to the Internet or a public library, research the roots of several of the Christmas symbols or rituals that are most important to you and your family in order to provide a deeper understanding of their meaning. If you cannot discover their true origin, assign a meaning that gives spiritual significance to how you desire to honor the coming of Christ. In the next few days, integrate what you have learned into your prayers.

DAY 24

Blessed Shipwreck

When you're really shipwrecked, you do really find what you want. When you're really on a desert island, you never find it a desert. If we were really besieged in this garden we'd find a hundred English birds and English berries that we never knew were here. If we were snowed up in this room, we'd be the better for reading scores of books in that bookcase that we don't even know are there; we'd have talks with each other, good terrible talks, that we shall go the grave without guessing; we'd find materials for everything...."

MANALIVE

LET EVERYTHING PRAISE THE LORD

> *Praise the LORD!*
> *Praise the LORD from the heavens;*
>   *praise him in the heights!*
> *Praise him, all his angels;*
>   *praise him, all his host!*
>
> *Praise him, sun and moon;*
>   *praise him, all you shining stars!*
> *Praise him, you highest heavens,*
>   *and you waters above the heavens!…*
>
> *Praise the LORD from the earth,*
>   *you sea monsters and all deeps,*
> *fire and hail, snow and frost,*
>   *stormy wind fulfilling his command!*
>
> *Mountains and all hills,*
>   *fruit trees and all cedars!*
> *Wild animals and all cattle,*
>   *creeping things and flying birds!*

PSALM 148:1–4, 7–10

PRAYER

O God, waken our sleepy senses to perceive your marvelous works in all that surrounds us. Let us endeavor to praise you for all your gifts—for the coldness of snow and swiftness of wind, for the tallness of trees and the greenness of grass, for the kindness of human eyes, and the music of a single voice.

ADVENT ACTION

Take a walk today, first through your home and then outside, making a mental list of things you normally take for granted (things as simple and common as a chair, lamppost, or hedge). Consider the deeper meaning of what you see—the gifts implied—and give God cheerful thanks. If you keep a journal, spend time there reflecting.

DAY 25

The Paradox of Charity

*C*harity is a paradox....Stated baldly, charity means one of two things—pardoning unpardonable acts, or loving unlovable people. But if we ask ourselves...what a sensible pagan would feel about such a subject, we shall probably be beginning at the bottom of it. A sensible pagan would say that there were some people one could forgive, and some one couldn't: a slave who stole wine could be laughed at; a slave who betrayed his benefactor could be killed, and cursed even after he was killed. Insofar as the act was pardonable, the man was pardonable. That again is rational, and even refreshing; but it is a dilution. It leaves no place for a pure horror of injustice....And it leaves no place for a mere tenderness for men as men, such as is the whole fascination of the charitable. Christianity came in...startlingly with a sword, and clove one thing from another. It divided the crime from the criminal. The criminal we must forgive unto seventy times seven. The crime we must not forgive at all. It was not enough that slaves who stole wine inspired partly anger and partly kindness. We must be much more angry with theft than before, and yet much kinder to thieves than before. There was room for wrath and love to run wild.

ORTHODOXY

SEVENTY TIMES SEVEN

Then Peter came and said to him, "Lord, if another member of the church sins against me, how often should I forgive? As many as seven times?" Jesus said to him, "Not seven times, but, I tell you, seventy times seven."

MATTHEW 18:21–22

PRAYER

Lord of Outrageous Grace, you showed Peter and you show us the stinginess of our forgiveness. Peter hoped for a lower number, six or perhaps five times to forgive his neighbor. We often settle for once, or not at all. How can we be as forgiving as you command? How can we, except by your grace, have the strength to offer ourselves again and again to those who offend us? Pour out your spirit on us, Lord Christ, and grant that we may one day stop counting altogether.

ADVENT ACTION

If someone offends you today, forgive that person. If you offend someone, ask for forgiveness. As you do either of these actions, say a silent prayer to God for His assistance.

One Sermon

*I*f I had one sermon to preach, it would be a sermon against Pride. The more I see of existence...the more I am convinced of the reality of the old religious thesis, that all evil began with some attempt at superiority; some moment when, as we might say, the very skies were cracked across like a mirror, because there was a sneer in Heaven.

THE COMMON MAN

THE PROUD HUMBLED

> *The haughty eyes of people shall be brought low,*
> *and the pride of everyone shall be humbled;*
> *and the LORD alone will be exalted*
> *in that day.*

> *For the LORD of hosts has a day*
> *against all that is proud and lofty,*
> *against all that is lifted up and high.*

> ISAIAH 2:11–12

PRAYER

Lord of Hosts, you will not suffer the prideful always. Over and over in your Word you tell us to be humble, but we so easily forget. Show us our hidden prides. Give us the courage to see them. And blot them out, we pray, that we might have a right opinion of ourselves and gladly glorify you, Exalted One, Humbler of the Prideful.

ADVENT ACTION

Sometimes we can't see the source of our pride. Our close friends, and especially fellow believers, however, can help. Before this day ends, arrange to have a conversation with someone whose confidence you trust. Ask the person this simple question, "What am I prideful about?" Prepare to listen without defensiveness. After the conversation with your friend, say a prayer asking God to reveal to you two things: (1) whether a true word has been spoken by your friend and, (2) if so, how to remove this source of pride.

DAY 27

Christmas Creations

*J*t is not so much old things as new things that a real Christmas might create. It might, for instance, create new games, if people were really driven to invent their own games. Most of the very old games began with the use of ordinary tools or furniture.

"THE SPIRIT OF CHRISTMAS," *THE THING: WHY I AM A CATHOLIC*

MAKER OF ALL THINGS

In the beginning was the Word, and the Word was with God, and the Word was God. He was in the beginning with God. All things came into being through him, and without him not one thing came into being.

JOHN 1:1–3b

PRAYER

Thank you, sovereign God, for creating us in your image, as co-creators, giving us the capacity to dream, imagine, and invent. Thank you for the blessings and benefits of human history and culture. Help us use wisely our technology; inspire our art. Thank you for the satisfaction of work well done. Thank you for new ideas that come to fruition. Thank you for the laughter of leisure. Let us use all our creativity and imagination to worship you this Advent and Christmas.

ADVENT ACTION

Using ordinary household or outdoor objects (the kind available to you), create a game to play (by yourself, if necessary; preferably with family, friends, or neighbors). Strive to make the game's objective more about celebration and enjoyment (purposely acting a little childish) than about who wins.

DAY 28

The Christ Child

The Christ-child lay on Mary's lap,
His hair was like a light.
(O weary, weary were the world,
But here is all aright.)

The Christ-child lay on Mary's breast
His hair was like a star.
(O stern and cunning are the kings,
But here the true hearts are.)

The Christ-child lay on Mary's heart,
His hair was like a fire.
(O weary, weary is the world,
But here the world's desire.)

The Christ-child stood on Mary's knee,
His hair was like a crown,
And all the flowers looked up at Him,
And all the stars looked down.

COLLECTED POETRY

THE BIRTH OF JESUS

Joseph also went from the town of Nazareth in Galilee to Judea, to the city of David called Bethlehem, because he was descended from the house and family of David. He went to be registered with Mary, to whom he was engaged and who was expecting a child....And she gave birth to her firstborn son and wrapped him in bands of cloth, and laid him in a manger....

LUKE 2:4–5, 7

PRAYER

Tenderly, frailly you came into our world Lord Jesus Christ, God as Baby, Eternal One as Infant. May the wonder of this event never lose its meaning, and may we always give you thanks and praise for this the most humble act in history.

ADVENT ACTION

Spend a few moments today looking at a nativity scene. Allow your imagination to enter this scene in the way that Chesterton does in his poem above. After you have finished looking, say a prayer of thanks to Jesus for entering the world in order to save it.

PART II

~~~~~~

Readings
for the
Twelve Days
of
Christmas

At the Back of Our Heart

*N*o other birth of a god or childhood of a sage seems to us to be Christmas or anything like Christmas. It is either too cold or too frivolous, or too formal and classical, or too simple and savage, or too occult and complicated. Not one of us, whatever his opinions, would ever go to such a scene with the sense that he was going home. He might admire it because it was poetical, or because it was philosophical, or any number of other things in separation; but not because it was itself. The truth is that there is a quite peculiar and individual character about the hold of this story on human nature; it is not in its psychological substance at all like a mere legend or the life of a great man....It does not exactly work outwards, adventurously, to the wonders to be found at the ends of the earth. It is rather something that surprises us from behind, from the hidden and personal part of our being....It is rather as if a man had found an inner room in the very heart of his own house, which he had never suspected; and seen a light from within. It is as if he found something at the back of his own heart that betrayed him into good.

THE EVERLASTING MAN

AT HOME NEAR THE MANGER

In that region there were shepherds living in the fields, keeping watch over their flock by night. Then an angel of the Lord stood before them, and the glory of the Lord shone around them, and they were terrified. But the angel said to them, "Do not be afraid; for see—I am bringing you good news of great joy for all the people: to you is born this day in the city of David a Savior, who is the Messiah, the Lord. This will be a sign for you: you will find a child wrapped in bands of cloth and lying in a manger."

LUKE 2:8–12

PRAYER

Lord, how secretly, how silently the wondrous gift of your Spirit is given! We invite you to cast out our cynicism and enter into our minds, wills, and affections, so that we might be born anew today. Inscribe your law on our minds that we might know it and keep it; mingle your love in all our doing; impart to our hearts the life of your Spirit. Good and gracious Lord, betray us into your goodness.

CHRISTMAS ACTION

Contemplation precedes every action. Every human action first forms in a thought. Sow seeds of contemplation this morning, watering them frequently with prayer throughout the day, attentive to how these seeds might flower into action. Begin by setting aside time early in the day for silent prayer. Determine how much time you can "sacrifice" to God. Twenty minutes twice a day is optimal; try seven minutes if that is all you can manage. Find a quiet place. Sit comfortably. Read the selections above from Chesterton and Luke several times aloud, and then remain silent. Set an alarm or use prayer beads if your schedule is an issue. If you find your mind wandering, when you catch yourself, repeat a single word: perhaps "Savior," or "Lord." At the end of this time, read the passage from Luke again meditatively. During the day, try to be aware of how to act more calmly, patiently, lovingly, and filled with faith.

DAY 2

Feast Days

$\mathcal{T}$he forms and rites of Christmas Day are meant merely to give the last push to people who are afraid to be festive. Father Christmas exists to haul us out of bed and make us partake of meals too beautiful to be called breakfasts.

ILLUSTRATED LONDON NEWS, JANUARY 8, 1910

INVITATION TO A BANQUET

Then Jesus said to him, "Someone gave a great dinner and invited many. At the time for the dinner he sent his slave to say to those who had been invited, 'Come, for everything is ready now.' But they all alike began to make excuses. The first said to him, 'I have bought a piece of land, and I must go out and see it; please accept my regrets.' Another said, 'I have bought five yoke of oxen, and I am going to try them out; please accept my regrets.' Another said, 'I have just been married, and therefore I cannot come.' So the slave returned and reported this to his master. Then the owner of the house became angry and said to his salve. 'Go out at once into the streets and lanes of the town and bring in the poor, the crippled, the blind, and the lame.' And the slave said, 'Sir, what you ordered has been done, and there is still room.' Then the master said to the slave, 'Go out into the roads and lanes, and compel people to come in, so that my house may be filled.'"

LUKE 14:16–23

PRAYER

Thank you, God of Light, for day and night and
    for change of seasons.
Thank you for everything artistic,
    for color combinations like green and red.
Thank you for food and spices
    that blend to romance our taste buds.
Thank you for the happiness of children and
    for the wisdom of old age; for the thrill
    of good music and for the music of good laughter.
Thank you, God of Love, for the blessing of family
    and friends and the opportunity we always have
    to befriend the hapless and hurting.

CHRISTMAS ACTION

Sometime this week create a Christmas Feast, a grand occasion to celebrate Christ's coming. It can be simple, but do it with family or friends, and if possible with flourish. Decorate; use your best dishes. Add elements of ritual or symbol: candles, music, a Christmas prayer, a time for reading stories aloud after the meal, or sharing a favorite Christmas memory around the table.

DAY 3

Irritable Guests

A Christmas dinner, as described by a modern minor poet, would almost certainly be a study in acute agony: the unendurable dullness of Uncle George; the cacophonous voice of Aunt Adelaide. But Chaucer, who sat down at the table with the Miller and the Pardoner, could have sat down to a Christmas dinner with the heaviest uncle or the shrillest aunt. He might have been amused at them, but he would never have been angered at them, and certainly he would never have insulted them in irritable little poems. And the reason was partly spiritual and partly practical; spiritual because he had, whatever his faults, a scheme of spiritual values in their right order, and knew that Christmas was more important than Uncle George's anecdotes; and practical because he had seen the great world of human beings, and knew that wherever a man wanders among men..., he will find that the world largely consists of Uncle Georges. This imaginative patience is the thing that men want [that is, "lack"] most in the modern Christmas.

"CHAUCER AND CHRISTMAS,"
ILLUSTRATED LONDON NEWS, DECEMBER 26, 1931

CHRISTIAN CLOTHING

As God's chosen ones, holy and beloved, clothe yourselves with compassion, kindness, humility, meekness, and patience. Bear with one another and, if anyone has a complaint against another, forgive each other; just as the Lord has forgiven you, so you also must forgive. Above all, clothe yourselves with love, which binds everything together in perfect harmony.

COLOSSIANS 3:12–14

PRAYER

So often, Jesus, I consider myself the center of the universe, where other people exist mainly as actors in my play—entering or exiting for my boredom or benefit. So often, Lord, I judge others carelessly: criticizing based on externals, carping because of a secret dissatisfaction that originates in me. Help me to act more generously and graciously to others, Lord of kindness, that I might see the best in them; indeed, that I might see you in them.

CHRISTMAS ACTION

Practice listening attentively to at least two people today (at work or at home)—especially people who might normally irritate you. Smile at the person as you listen. Discover a good characteristic in them and give God thanks for that quality.

DAY 4

A Child Is Born

And the rafters of toil still are gilded
With the dawn of the stars of the heart,
And the wise men draw near in the twilight,
Who are weary of learning and art,
And the face of the tyrant is darkened,
His spirit is torn,
For a new king is enthroned; yea, the sternest,
A child is born.

And the mother still joys for the whispered
First stir of unspeakable things,
Still feels that high moment unfurling
Red glory of Gabriel's wings.
Still the babe of an hour is a master
Whom angels adorn,
Emmanuel, prophet, anointed,
A child is born.

FROM "NATIVITY," *COLLECTED POETRY*

WORDS TO PONDER

When the angels had left them and gone into heaven, the shepherds said to one another, "Let us go now to Bethlehem and see this thing that has taken place, which the Lord has made known to us." So they went with haste and found Mary and Joseph, and the child lying in the manger. When they saw this, they made known what had been told them about this child; and all who heard it were amazed at what the shepherds told them. But Mary treasured all these words and pondered them in her heart.

LUKE 2:15–19

PRAYER

Lord Jesus, you amazed many at your birth. May we not fail, even at our distance in time, to marvel at these events. Let us share the shepherds' excitement at their encounter with angels. Let their story be our story, too. And let us ponder this miraculous tale, just as Mary did, holding each word close, as close as our own hearts.

CHRISTMAS ACTION

There are two accounts of Christ's birth (see Matthew 1:18—2:1–23; Luke 2:1–20). Read each one slowly, meditatively. Try to imagine that you are reading the story for the first time. What details stand out to you? What parts of this story do you especially treasure?

DAY 5

Omnipotent Weakness

$\mathcal{I}$t is no more inevitable to connect God with an infant than to connect gravitation with a kitten. It has been created in our minds by Christmas because we are Christians, because we are psychological Christians even when we are not theological ones....Omnipotence and impotence, or divinity and infancy, do definitely make a sort of epigram which a million repetitions cannot turn into a platitude. It is not unreasonable to call it unique. Bethlehem is emphatically a place where extremes meet.

THE EVERLASTING MAN

DIVINE DESCENDING

For you know the generous act of our Lord Jesus Christ, that
though he was rich, yet for your sakes he became poor, so
that by his poverty you might become rich.

2 CORINTHIANS 8:9

PRAYER

Thank you, Triune God, for the mystery of your Incarnation. Thank you for the mystery that grows more mysterious as we grasp it better. Thank you, Christ, for assuming the burden of our mortal flesh, for hallowing and redeeming it. Graft into us a refusal to hide from our weaknesses, offering them instead to you as an opportunity to fill us with the divine strength of your Holy Spirit.

CHRISTMAS ACTION

Considering the people in your life at home and at work, imagine a hypothetical ladder of power, with those above and below you. Where do you fit in this configuration? Name the key people in your life with whom you struggle for power. Determine today, first, to grant dignity and a voice to those people below you on the ladder; pray for any above you on the ladder as you encounter them and make an effort to say nothing today that advances your own self-image.

Homeless and at Home

A child in a foul stable,
Where the beast feed and foam;
Only where He was homeless
Are you and I at home;
We have hands that fashion and heads that know,
But our hearts we lost—how long ago!
In a place no chart nor ship can show
Under the sky's dome.

This world is wild as an old wive's tale,
And strange the plain things are,
The earth is enough and the air is enough
For our wonder and our war;
But our rest is as far as the fire-drake swings
And our peace is put in impossible things
Where clashed and thundered unthinkable wings
Round an incredible star.

To an open house in the evening
Home shall men come,
To an older place than Eden
And a taller town than Rome.
To the end of the way of the wandering star,
To the things that cannot be and that are,
To the place where God was homeless
And all men are at home.

FROM "THE HOUSE OF CHRISTMAS," *COLLECTED POETRY*

THE PLACE WHERE THE STAR STOPPED

When they had heard the king, [the wise men] set out; and there, ahead of them, went the star they had seen at its rising, until it stopped over the place where the child was. When they saw that the star had stopped, they were overwhelmed with joy. On entering the house, they saw the child with Mary his mother; and they knelt down and paid him homage. Then, opening their treasure chests, they offered him gifts of gold, frankincense, and myrrh.

MATTHEW 2:9–11

PRAYER

Lord Jesus Christ, you came into our world as a baby, but clues to your identity were scattered across the landscape. Angels sang to shepherds. Wise men followed a star. They arrived at your side and knelt down to give you gifts. May we witness signs this Christmas season and be drawn to you, Heavenly Infant, God in a Manger. May the wonder of those miraculous days, though long removed from us, still reverberate through time. Let us also come and adore you.

CHRISTMAS ACTION

If you are keeping a journal, write an entry in which you summarize the Christmas story without looking back at the biblical texts. After your summary, focus more closely on one specific character in this story. Try to imagine what it would have been like to have accompanied Christ's birth. Do so through the eyes of Mary or Joseph, the shepherds, the Wise Men, or any other member of this marvelous tale.

DAY 7

Outlaw King

*C*hrist was not only born on the level of the world, but even lower than the world....But in the riddle of Bethlehem it was heaven that was under the earth. There is in that alone the touch of a revolution, as of the world turned upside down. It would be vain to attempt to say anything adequate, or anything new, about the change which this conception of a deity born like an outcast or even an outlaw had upon the whole conception of law and its duties to the poor and outcast. It is profoundly true to say that after that moment there could be no slaves....Individuals became important, in a sense in which no instruments can be important. A man could not be a means to an end, at any rate to any other man's end.

THE EVERLASTING MAN

GOOD NEWS TO THE POOR

> *He unrolled the scroll and found the place where it*
> *was written:*
>> *"The Spirit of the Lord is upon me,*
>>> *because he has anointed me*
>>>> *to bring good news to the poor.*
>> *He has sent me to proclaim release to the captives*
>> *and recovery of sight to the blind,*
>>>> *to let the oppressed go free,*
>> *to proclaim the year of the Lord's favor."*

LUKE 4:17b–19

PRAYER

Thank you, Son of Man, for becoming poor that we might become spiritually rich. Thank you for appearing clothed in lowly humility thereby ennobling all common people. May your example of meekness motivate us toward solidarity with the world's poor and toward a commitment to pursue social justice.

CHRISTMAS ACTION

Begin this task by asking God to direct you in and through this action. Set aside time in your calendar during the next two weeks to serve the poor in some way. Ascertain a local ministry that needs volunteers—for example, Habitat for Humanity, a food pantry or shelter, an orphanage, or a home for the mentally challenged. Contact the organization and find out what their needs are; if possible, schedule a time to work with them. As you are working in this setting and as you encounter people in need, repeat this phrase: "Lord Jesus Christ, allow me to serve you."

DAY 8

Blessed Boomerang

*C*hristmas is quite certainly the most interesting thing in England to-day. It is the last living link between all that remains of the most delicate religious devotion and all that exists of the coarsest town vulgarity....The return of old things in new times, by an established and automatic machinery, is the permanent security of men who like to be sane. The greatest of all blessings is the boomerang. And all the healthiest things we know are boomerangs—that is, they are things that return. Sleep is a boomerang. We fling it from us at morning, and it knocks us down again at night. Daylight is a boomerang. We see it at the end of the day disappearing in the distance; and at the beginning of the next day we see it come back and break the sky....The same sort of sensational sanity (truly to be called sensational because it braces and strengthens all the sensations) is given by the return of religious and social festivals. To have such an institution as a Christmas is, I will say not to make an accident inevitable, but I will say to make an adventure recurrent—and therefore, in one sense, to make an adventure everlasting. A practice like that of Christmas is, therefore, much the most practical way of resisting the meaningless modern fancy of perpetually advancing into the white fog of a formless future.

"CHRISTMAS VERSUS THE FUTURE,"
ILLUSTRATED LONDON NEWS, DECEMBER 20, 1913

JESUS BOOMERANG

Give ear, O my people, to my teaching;
*   incline your ears to the words of my mouth.*
I will open my mouth in a parable;
*   I will utter dark sayings from of old,*
things that we have heard and known,
*   that our ancestors have told us.*
We will not hide them from their children;
*   we will tell to the coming generation*
the glorious deeds of the LORD, and his might,
*   and the wonders that he has done.*

PSALM 78:1–4

PRAYER

Lord, cause the sacred history of Israel and your church to come alive for us. Let us perceive your glorious deeds, the wonders you have performed to wake us from spiritual slumber. Let the lives of the saints inspire us. Let Christmas be for us an adventure this year, a way of returning to the solid foundations of our faith. Show us, Gracious God, how you have been present in our own personal histories, how you have watched over us through good times and bad.

CHRISTMAS ACTION

On a piece of paper, draw two parallel lines, the top line representing high points in your spiritual journey, the bottom line representing low points. As if this were a time line, place the half dozen or so major spiritual turning points in your life—either positive or negative. Think back over those experiences or events. Where was God? If God seemed absent at times, can you imagine Jesus, who suffered so much while on earth, silently beside you, entering into past sufferings with you? When unpleasant things happen this week, acknowledge God's presence even in the midst of what is disagreeable. Say, "Lord, come be with me now."

The Wise Men

The Child that was ere worlds begun—
(...We need but walk a little way...
We need but see a latch undone...)
The Child that played with moon and sun
Is playing with a little hay.

The house from which the heavens are fed,
The old strange house that is our own,
Where tricks of words are never said,
And Mercy is as plain as bread,
And honor is as hard as stone.

Go humbly; humble as the skies,
And low and large and fierce the Star,
So very near the Manger lies
That we may travel far.

FROM "THE WISE MEN," COLLECTED POETRY

JOURNEY OF THE WISE MEN

In the time of King Herod, after Jesus was born in Bethlehem of Judea, wise men from the East came to Jerusalem, asking "Where is the child who has been born king of the Jews? For we observed his star at its rising, and have come to pay him homage."

MATTHEW 2:1–2

PRAYER

Jesus, Holy Child, your birth was signaled by a star, so that those who sought you could find you. Help us in our journey to your manger. Light the way, as you did for the wise men millennia ago, for we too wish to pay you homage.

CHRISTMAS ACTION

If the weather permits, go for a walk tonight. Choose a place where there is the least amount of artificial light so you can enjoy the sight of the stars.

DAY 10

Shaking the Palaces

*U*nless we understand the presence of that enemy, we shall not only miss the point of Christianity, but even miss the point of Christmas....By the very nature of the story the rejoicings in the cavern were rejoicings in a fortress or an outlaw's den; properly understood it is not unduly flippant to say they were rejoicings in a dug-out. It is not only true that such a subterranean chamber was a hiding-place from enemies; and that the enemies were already scouring the stony plain that lay above it like a sky. It is not only that the very horse-hoofs of Herod might in that sense have passed like thunder over the sunken head of Christ. It is also that there is in that image a true idea of an outpost, of a piercing through the rock and an entrance into an enemy territory. There is in this buried divinity an idea of undermining the world; of shaking the towers and palaces from below; even as

Herod the great king felt that earthquake under him and swayed with his swaying palace.

THE EVERLASTING MAN

FOOLISH WISDOM AND WEAK POWER

Where is the one who is wise? Where is the scribe? Where is the debater of this age? Has not God made foolish the wisdom of the world? For since, in the wisdom of God, the world did not know God through wisdom, God decided, through the foolishness of our proclamation, to save those who believe. For Jews demand signs and Greeks desire wisdom, but we proclaim Christ crucified, a stumbling block to Jews and foolishness to Gentiles, but to those who are the called, both Jews and Greeks, Christ the power of God and the wisdom of God. For God's foolishness is wiser than human wisdom, and God's weakness is stronger than human strength.

1 CORINTHIANS 1:20–25

PRAYER

God of all Providence, defend us from our enemies and deliver us from engaging in schemes of evil. Shelter us from those who would harm us—in body, mind, or spirit—and shield us against those forces in our culture that would entice us to harm others. Surround, guard, and guide us in the way of peace that we might sow seeds of peace. Let us stand strong against every form of oppression. Continually knock on the doors of our consciences that we might open the door, give welcome to your Spirit, and take seriously the course of peace you propose.

CHRISTMAS ACTION

In prayer today, ask God to help you recall someone who has hurt you. Ask God to help you forgive them, as he has forgiven you in Christ Jesus. The saying is true that it takes two to make peace, but only one to take the first step. Can you discern a way to offer to this person a sign of your forgiveness? Perhaps you could visit them or mail a gift; perhaps you could call or send a card. If the pain is still too fresh for you to embrace, write them a letter describing both the offense they caused and your forgiveness. Put the letter in an envelope with their name on it, but do not address it yet. Place the letter in prominent relation to some religious symbol in your home—near an icon, crèche, or Bible. Each time you come across it this week, ask God to remove the sting from your heart and to grant you grace to forgive this person.

DAY 11

The Neglected Child

The teachers in the Temple
They did not lift their eyes
For the blazing star of Bethlehem
Or the Wise men grown wise.

They heeded jot and tittle,
The heeded not a jot
The rending voice of Ramah
And the children that were not.

Or how the panic of the poor
Choked all the field with flight,
Or how the red sword of the rich
Ran ravening through the night.

They made their notes; while naked
And monstrous and obscene
A tyrant bathed in all the blood
Of men that might have been.

But they did chide Our Lady
And tax her for this thing,
That she had lost Him for a time
And sought him sorrowing.

COLLECTED POETRY

JESUS IN THE TEMPLE

Now every year his parents went to Jerusalem for the festival of the Passover. And when he was twelve years old, they went up as usual for the festival. When the festival was ended and they started to return, the boy Jesus stayed behind in Jerusalem, but his parents did not know it. Assuming that he was in the group of travelers, they went a day's journey. Then they started to look for him among their relatives and friends. When they did not find him, they returned to Jerusalem to search for him. After three days they found him in the temple, sitting among the teachers, listening to them and asking questions.

LUKE 2:41–46

PRAYER

Jesus, we sometimes lose sight of you, as your mother and father did on their way home from Jerusalem. Help us when we don't know where you are. Teach us where to look for you, that we may have you again in our company.

CHRISTMAS ACTION

Reread the poem by Chesterton above. In what ways have you acted like the teachers in the Temple who neglected important matters but did not fail to criticize another? Resolve to not judge others. Instead, offer help to those who need it.

DAY 12

The Living Church

The Christian Church in its practical relation to my soul is a living teacher, not a dead one. It not only certainly taught me yesterday, but will almost certainly teach me tomorrow. Once I saw suddenly the meaning of the shape of the cross; some day I may see suddenly the meaning of the shape of the mitre. One fine morning I saw why windows were pointed; some fine morning I may see why priests were shaven....The man who lives in contact with what he believes to be a living Church is a man always expecting...to see some truth that he has never seen before.

ORTHODOXY

TEACH ONE ANOTHER

Let the word of Christ dwell in you richly; teach and admonish one another in all wisdom; and with gratitude in your hearts sing psalms, hymns, and spiritual songs to God. And whatever you do, in word or deed, do everything in the name of the Lord Jesus, giving thanks to God the Father through him.

COLOSSIANS 3:16–17

PRAYER

Open us, Lord, to further lessons about you and your church. Help us to learn from one another, never believing that we have all the answers or that new answers might not come from unexpected places. Make us expectant for the unexpected, Eternal Teacher, and help us to be attentive students in the miraculous classroom that is your world.

CHRISTMAS ACTION

Does your church have a Bible study or catechetical class? If it does, try attending a session or two and learn what you can from the leader and the other members of the class.

PART III

~~~~~~

Formats
for
Nightly Prayer
and
Reading

Formats for Nightly Prayer and Reading

THE PURPOSE OF PRESENTING these two optional formats for nightly readings and prayer is to offer different ways to use the material in this book for group or individual prayer. Of course, there are other ways in which to use this book—for example, as a meditative daily reader or as a guide for a prayer journal—but the following familiar liturgical formats provide a structure that can be used in a variety of contexts.

FORMAT 1

OPENING PRAYER

The observance begins with these words:

> *God, come to my assistance.*
> *Lord, make haste to help me.*

followed by:

> *Glory to the Father, and to the Son,*
> *and to the Holy Spirit, as it was in the beginning,*
> *is now, and will be, for ever. Amen. Alleluia!*

EXAMINATION OF CONSCIENCE

If this observance is being prayed individually, an examination of conscience may be included. Here is a short examination of conscience; you may, of course, use your own preferred method.

1. Place yourself in a quiet frame of mind.
2. Review your life since your last confession.
3. Reflect on the Ten Commandments and any sins against these commandments.
4. Reflect on the words of the gospel, especially Jesus' commandment to love your neighbor as yourself.
5. Ask yourself these questions: How have I been unkind in thoughts, words, and actions? Am I refusing to forgive anyone? Do I despise any group or person? Am I a prisoner of fear, anxiety, worry, guilt, inferiority, or hatred of myself?

PENITENTIAL RITE (OPTIONAL)

If a group of people are praying in unison, a penitential rite from the *Roman Missal* may be used:

Presider: You were sent to heal the contrite of heart:
Lord, have mercy.

All: Lord, have mercy.

Presider: You came to call sinners:
Christ, have mercy.

All: Christ, have mercy.

Presider: You are seated at the right hand of the Father to intercede for us:
Lord, have mercy.

All: Lord, have mercy.

Presider: May almighty God have mercy on us, forgive us our sins, and bring us to everlasting life.

All: Amen.

HYMN: "O COME, O COME, EMMANUEL"

A hymn is now sung or recited. This Advent hymn is a paraphrase of the great "O" Antiphons written in the twelfth century and translated by John Mason Neale in 1852.

O come, O come, Emmanuel,
And ransom captive Israel;
That mourns in lonely exile here,
Until the Son of God appear.

Refrain: Rejoice! Rejoice!
             O Israel! To thee shall come, Emmanuel!

O come, thou wisdom, from on high,
And order all things far and nigh;
To us the path of knowledge show,
And teach us in her ways to go.

Refrain

O come, O come, thou Lord of might,
Who to thy tribes on Sinai's height
In ancient times did give the law,
In cloud, and majesty, and awe.

Refrain

O come, thou rod of Jesse's stem,
From ev'ry foe deliver them
That trust thy mighty power to save,
And give them vict'ry o'er the grave.

Refrain

O come, thou key of David, come,
And open wide our heav'nly home,
Make safe the way that leads on high,
That we no more have cause to sigh.

Refrain

O come, thou Dayspring from on high,
And cheer us by thy drawing nigh;
Disperse the gloomy clouds of night
And death's dark shadow put to flight.

Refrain

O come, Desire of nations, bind
In one the hearts of all mankind;
Bid every strife and quarrel cease
And fill the world with heaven's peace.

Refrain

PSALM 27:7–14—GOD STANDS BY US IN DANGERS

Hear, O LORD, when I cry aloud,
    be gracious to me and answer me!
"Come," my heart says, "seek his face!"
    Your face, LORD, do I seek.
    Do not hide your face from me.

Do not turn your servant away in anger,
    you who have been my help.
Do not cast me off, do not forsake me,
    O God of my salvation!
If my father and mother forsake me,
    the LORD will take me up.

Teach me your way, O LORD,
    and lead me on a level path
    because of my enemies.
Do not give me up to the will of my adversaries,
    for false witnesses have risen against me,
    and they are breathing out violence.

I believe that I shall see the goodness of the LORD
    in the land of the living.
Wait for the LORD;
        be strong, and let your heart take courage;
        wait for the LORD!

RESPONSE

I long to see your face, O Lord. You are my light and my help. Do not turn away from me.

SCRIPTURE READING

Read silently or have a presider proclaim the Scripture of the day that is selected.

RESPONSE

Come and set us free, Lord God of power and might. Let your face shine on us and we will be saved.
    Glory to the Father, and to the Son,
    and to the Holy Spirit, as it was in the beginning,
    is now, and will be for ever. Amen.

SECOND READING

Read the excerpt from G. K. Chesterton for the day selected.

CANTICLE OF SIMEON

Lord, now you let your servant go in peace;
    your word has been fulfilled:
My own eyes have seen the salvation
    which you have prepared in the sight of every people:

A light to reveal you to the nations
    and the glory of your people Israel.
Glory to the Father, and to the Son, and to the Holy Spirit,
as it was in the beginning, is now, and will be for ever.
Amen.

PRAYER

Say the prayer that follows the day's selected excerpt from
G. K. Chesterton.

BLESSING

May the Lord grant us a restful night and a peaceful death.
Amen.

MARIAN ANTIPHON

Loving mother of the Redeemer,
    gate of heaven, star of the sea,
        assist your people who have fallen yet strive to rise
            again.
To the wonderment of nature you bore your Creator,
    yet remained a virgin after as before.
You who received Gabriel's joyful greeting,
    have pity on us poor sinners.

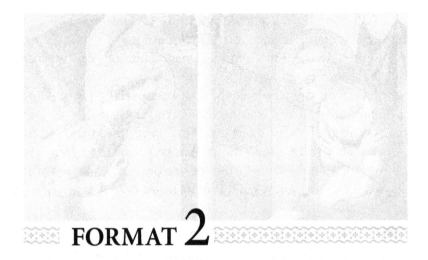

FORMAT 2

OPENING PRAYER

The observance begins with these words:

> *God, come to my assistance.*
> *Lord, make haste to help me.*

followed by:

> *Glory to the Father, and to the Son,*
> *and to the Holy Spirit, as it was in the beginning,*
> *is now, and will be, for ever. Amen. Alleluia!*

EXAMINATION OF CONSCIENCE

If this observance is being prayed individually, an examination of conscience may be included. Here is a short examination of conscience; you may, of course, use your own preferred method.

1. Place yourself in a quiet frame of mind.
2. Review your life since your last confession.
3. Reflect on the Ten Commandments and any sins against these commandments.
4. Reflect on the words of the gospel, especially Jesus' commandment to love your neighbor as yourself.
5. Ask yourself these questions: How have I been unkind in thoughts, words, and actions? Am I refusing to forgive anyone? Do I despise any group or person? Am I a prisoner of fear, anxiety, worry, guilt, inferiority, or hatred of myself?

PENITENTIAL RITE (OPTIONAL)

If a group of people are praying in unison, a penitential rite from the *Roman Missal* may be used:

All: I confess to almighty God
and to you, my brothers and sisters,
that I have greatly sinned,
in my thoughts and in my words,
in what I have done and in what I have failed to do,
through my fault, through my fault,
through my most grievous fault;
therefore I ask blessed Mary ever-Virgin,
all the Angels and Saints,
and you, my brothers and sisters,
to pray for me to the Lord our God.

Presider: May almighty God have mercy on us,
forgive us our sins,
and bring us to everlasting life.

All: Amen.

Hymn: "Behold, a Rose"

A hymn is now sung or recited. This traditional hymn was composed in German in the fifteenth century. It is sung to the melody of the familiar "Lo, How a Rose E're Blooming."

> Behold, a rose of Judah
> From tender branch has sprung,
> From Jesse's lineage coming,
> As men of old have sung.
> It came a flower bright
> Amid the cold of winter,
> When half spent was the night.
>
> Isaiah has foretold it
> In words of promise sure,
> And Mary's arms enfold it,
> A virgin meek and pure.
> Through God's eternal will
> She bore for men a savior
> At midnight calm and still.

Psalm 40:1–8—Thanksgiving for Deliverance

> I waited patiently for the LORD;
>> he inclined to me and heard my cry.
> He drew me up from the desolate pit,
>> out of the miry bog,
> and set my feet upon a rock,
>> making my steps secure.
> He put a new song in my mouth,
>> a song of praise to our God.
> Many will see and fear,
>> and put their trust in the LORD.

Happy are those who make
    the LORD their trust,
who do not turn to the proud,
    to those who go astray after false gods.
You have multiplied, O LORD, my God,
    your wondrous deeds and your thoughts toward us;
    none can compare with you.
Were I to proclaim and tell of them,
    they would be more than can be counted.

Sacrifice and offering you do not desire,
    but you have given me an open ear.
Burnt offering and sin offering
    you have not required.
Then I said, "Here I am;
    in the scroll of the book it is written of me.
I delight to do your will, O my God;
    your law is within my heart."

RESPONSE

May all who seek after you be glad in the Lord, may those who find
your salvation say with continuous praise, "Great is the Lord!"

SCRIPTURE READING

Read silently or have a presider proclaim the Scripture of the day
that is selected.

RESPONSE

Lord, you who were made obedient unto death, teach us to always do the Father's will, so that, sanctified by the holy obedience that joins us to your sacrifice, we can count on your immense love in times of sorrow.

Glory to the Father, and to the Son,
and to the Holy Spirit, as it was in the beginning,
is now, and will be, for ever. Amen.

SECOND READING

Read silently or have a presider read the words of G. K. Chesterton for the day selected.

CANTICLE OF SIMEON

Lord, now you let your servant go in peace;
  your word has been fulfilled:
My own eyes have seen the salvation
  which you have prepared in the sight of every people:
A light to reveal you to the nations
  and the glory of your people Israel.
Glory to the Father, and to the Son, and to the Holy Spirit,
as it was in the beginning, is now, and will be for ever.
Amen.

PRAYER

Recite the prayer that follows the excerpt from G. K. Chesterton for the day selected.

BLESSING

Lord, give our bodies restful sleep and let the work we have done today bear fruit in eternal life. Watch over us as we rest in your peace. Amen.

MARIAN ANTIPHON

Hail, holy Queen, mother of mercy,
    our life, our sweetness, and our hope.
To you do we cry,
    poor banished children of Eve.
To you do we send up our sighs,
    mourning and weeping in this vale of tears.
Turn then, most gracious advocate,
    your eyes of mercy toward us,
    and after this exile
    show to us the blessed fruit of your womb, Jesus.
O clement, O loving,
O sweet Virgin Mary. Amen.

Sources and Acknowledgments

The *Collected Works of G. K. Chesterton,* an ongoing project published by Ignatius Press, attempts to make available in one source all of Chesterton's published writings. At present, the series includes thirty-seven volumes. Material excerpted for this book can be found in that excellent series, with the exception of the following:

Chesterton, G. K. "A Charge of Irreverence." In *Lunacy and Letters,* edited by Dorothy Collins. New York: Sheed and Ward, 1958.

———. *Autobiography.* New York: Sheed and Ward, 1936. Used with permission of A P Watt Ltd. on behalf of The Royal Literary Fund.

———. *Chaucer.* New York: Sheed and Ward, 1956. Used with permission of A P Watt Ltd. on behalf of The Royal Literary Fund.

———. *The Common Man.* New York: Sheed and Ward, 1950. Used with permission of A P Watt Ltd. on behalf of The Royal Literary Fund.

———. *The Defendant.* New York: Dodd, Mead and Co., 1902.

———. *The Everlasting Man.* New York: Dodd, Mead & Co., 1925. Used with permission of A P Watt Ltd. on behalf of The Royal Literary Fund.

———. "On the Thrills of Boredom." In *All Is Grist.* North Stratford, NH: Ayer Company Publishers, 2000. Used with permission of A P Watt Ltd. on behalf of The Royal Literary Fund.

———. "The New War on Christmas." In *Brave New Family*, edited by Alvaro de Silva. San Francisco: Ignatius, 1990.

———. *The Outline of Sanity*. London: Methuen and Co., 1926. Used with permission of A P Watt Ltd. on behalf of The Royal Literary Fund.

———. "The Red Angel." In *Tremendous Trifles*. London: Methuen and Co., 1929.

———. *Saint Francis of Assisi*. Garden City, NY: Doubleday and Co., 1954. Used with permission of A P Watt Ltd. on behalf of The Royal Literary Fund.

———. *The Thing: Why I Am a Catholic*. New York: Dodd, Mead, & Do., 1946. Used with permission of A P Watt Ltd. on behalf of The Royal Literary Fund.

———. *Varied Types*. New York: Dodd, Mead and Co., 1908.